Dressed for the races in an accordion-pleated,
square-shouldered bolero jacket, embroidered
blouse and high-waisted, straight skirt, 1933.

Elsa Schiaparelli in the trompe-l'oeil sweater,
worn over a trumpet skirt, that launched her
celebrity as a designer, 1927.

PLATE 1

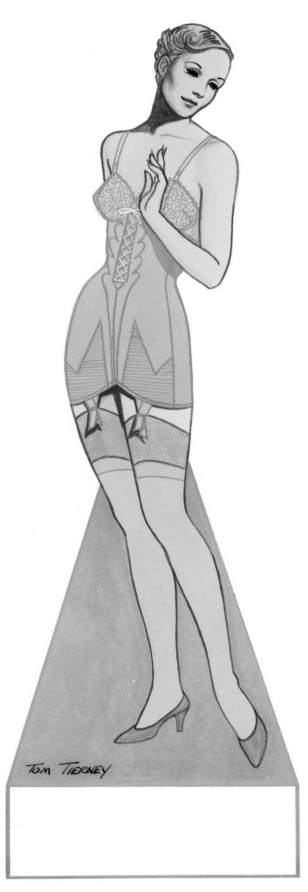

Corset designed for Mae West in *Every Day's a Holiday*, 1937.

Swimsuit of rayon twill, 1949.

PLATE 2

Do not cut out white area between arm and body.

Spectator sports costume of thin plaid tweed and crepe de chine, 1930.

Beach costume made of half-dresses, each with one armhole, tied at the side like an apron, 1930.

PLATE 3

A gown inspired by the Directoire, worn with
slave bracelets, 1931.

Crepe gown with velvet spencer, 1931.

PLATE 4

Do not cut out white area between arm and body.

Sports suit of deeply crinkled string-colored woolen crepe. The corselet skirt mounts high to meet a short-sleeved linen blouse, 1932.

Formal gown of matvelva with sleeves of ostrich feathers glycerinized to give them extra luster, 1932.

PLATE 5

Do not cut out white area
between arm and body.

Broadcloth coat over crepe de chine dress in a
broken plaid, 1933.

Party dress of cloth underskirt topped by flecked
linen in a bustle treatment, 1934.

PLATE 6

Do not cut out white area
between arm and body.

Jersey spring suit in the bird silhouette,
with wing-revers, 1934.

Militaristic suit of horseguards' cloth with wool-
fringe epaulets and cuffs, oversize buttons and
velvet hood collar. Hair worn in a coarse net
under the disk hat, 1935.

PLATE 7

Draped and molded satin "column" dress, 1935.

Velvet evening ensemble with flat pleats trimming the jacket and large godets in the front of the skirt, 1936.

PLATE 8

Do not cut out white area between
arm and body.

Dress of satin with a tulle ruffle on
the skirt, 1936.

Fitted coat with a yoke cut across the bosom and
black leather lovebird buttons, 1936.

PLATE 9

Bias-cut satin wedding gown with a veil embroidered with seashells, 1937.

PLATE 10

Do not cut out white area between arm and body.

Dinner dress of coarse linen, the jacket with woman's head, designed by Jean Cocteau, embroidered with hair of gold bugle beads and sequins, 1937.

Costume for Mae West in *Every Day's a Holiday* (released 1938). Schiaparelli and West never met, a dress form having been sent to Paris. The form inspired the shape of the bottle for Shocking perfume.

PLATE 11

Evening gown with shocking-pink balloon
sleeves, 1938. The print of the dress, designed by
Vertès, depicts fairground animals.

Woolen cape emblazoned with gold, 1938.

PLATE 12

Surrealist gown and headdress of medieval in-
spiration with bolero jacket and full-length
gloves, 1938. The print suggests a Rorschach test.

Cape and dress of geometric design with bold
color contrast, 1939.

PLATE 13

Do not cut out white area
between arm and body.

Satin bustle dress striped with
satin ribbon, 1939.

Black velvet evening suit trimmed with gold
tinsel and mirrors; plastic buttons in the shape
of Baroque women's heads, 1939.

PLATE 14

Do not cut out white
area between arm and body.

Crepe gown, 1940.

Satin bodice of shocking pink trimmed with
black-beaded embroidery, worn over a black
bouffant skirt, 1950.

PLATE 15

Satin cocktail dress and cap, 1952.

Costume for Zsa Zsa Gabor as Jane Avril in the
motion picture *Moulin Rouge*, 1953.

PLATE 16